I Like Soccer

Angela Aylmore

www.heinemann.co.uk/library
Visit our website to find out more information about Heinemann Library books.

To order:
 Phone 44 (0) 1865 888066
Send a fax to 44 (0) 1865 314091
Visit the Heinemann Bookshop at www.heinemann.co.uk/library to browse our
catalogue and order online.

First published in Great Britain by Heinemann Library,
Halley Court, Jordan Hill, Oxford OX2 8EJ, part
of Harcourt Education. Heinemann is a registered
trademark of Harcourt Education Ltd.

© Harcourt Education Ltd 2007
First published in paperback 2008
The moral right of the proprietor has been asserted.

Editorial: Dan Nunn and Sarah Chappelow
Design: Joanna Hinton-Malivoire
Picture research: Erica Newbery
Production: Duncan Gilbert

Origination: Chroma Graphics (Overseas) Pte. Ltd
Printed and bound in China, China by South
China Printing Co. Ltd.

ISBN 978 0 431 10955 8 (hardback)
11 10 09 08 07
10 9 8 7 6 5 4 3 2 1

ISBN 978 0 431 10964 0 (paperback)
12 11 10 09 08
10 9 8 7 6 5 4 3 2 1

British Library Cataloguing in Publication Data
Aylmore, Angela
  I like soccer. - (Things I like)
  1. Soccer - Juvenile literature
  I. Title
  796.3'34
A full catalogue record for this book is available from
the British Library.

Acknowledgements
The publishers would like to thank the following for
permission to reproduce photographs: Alamy pp.
18–19 (Stephen Roberts), **21** (The Photolibrary Wales);
Corbis pp. **5** (John Fortunato), **22** (child with ball,
John Fortunato Photography); Getty Images pp. **4–5**
(Photodisc; boy with football, Photographer's Choice),
6 (Blend Images), **8** (Photodisc), **9** (Pascal Rondeau/
Allsport Concepts), **10–11** (Livia Corona/Taxi), **12**
(Kevin Fitzgerald/The Image Bank), **14** (Southern Stock/
Photonica), **16–17** (Juan Silva), **22** (goal celebration,
Juan Silva; players in kit, Livia Corona/Taxi; goal scoring,
Southern Stock); Jupiter Images pp. **7** (Lilly Dong/
Botanica), **13** (Brand X Pictures), **15** (Banana Stock), **20**
(Image Source).

Cover photograph of a footballer reproduced with
permission of Jupiter Images (Maurizio Borsari).

Every effort has been made to contact copyright holders
of any material reproduced in this book. Any omissions
will be rectified in subsequent printings if notice is given
to the publishers.

Contents

Some words are shown in bold, **like this**. You can find out what they mean by looking in the Glossary.

Sport

I like sport.

My favourite sport is soccer.

I like to watch soccer on the television.

I like to play soccer too.

The kit

shirt

13

shorts

socks

boots

This is what people wear
when they play soccer.

If they play in **goal** they also wear gloves.

There are eleven people
in a soccer team. They
all wear the same kit.

Playing Soccer

The **referee** makes sure
the teams play the game
properly.

The referee blows a
whistle to start the game.

Two teams play in a game.
Everyone tries to score a goal.

At half-time all the players have a break.

I like it when my team wins. But even if we lose, I still like soccer!

Going to u match

Sometimes I go to a soccer stadium to watch a match.

The field we play on is called the **pitch**. The seats in the stadium are called the **stands**.

The **fans** sit in the stands.
Everyone cheers when
our team scores a goal!

Do you like soccer?

Now you know why I like soccer! Do you like soccer too?

Glossary

fans people who support a
soccer team

goal when a team scores. It is also the
place where players must put the ball
in order to score.

pitch the playing area

referee person who makes sure that
the rules are followed in a game

stand place where the fans sit
at a soccer match

Find out more

Complete Soccer School, Gill Harvey
(Usborne Publishing, 2000)

Football: Rules of the Game, Jim Kelman
(Hodder Wayland, 2006)

Soccer, Hugh Hornby
(Dorling Kindersley, 2005)

Index